30119 028 740 38 1   D0551949

What is Race? Who are Racists? Why Does Skin Colour Matter? And other Big Questions

Claire Heuchan & Nikesh Shukla

WAYLAND
www.waylandbooks.co.uk

For every child who has struggled to find the answers to all of their questions about race. (C.H.)

Published in paperback in Great Britain in 2020 by Wayland

Claire Heuchan and Nikesh Shukla have asserted their rights to be identified as the Author of this Work.

Text Copyright © Claire Heuchan and Nikesh Shukla, 2018
Contributor text Copyright ©: Derek Owusu's text pp14-15 © Derek Owusu, 2018; Inua Ellams' text pp18-19 © Inua Ellams, 2018; Asim Chaudhry's text pp23-25 © Asim Chaudhry, 2018; Wei Ming Kam's text pp28-29 © Wei Ming Kam, 2018; Becky Olaniyi's text pp30-31 © Becky Olaniyi, 2018; Nadine Aisha Jassat's text pp28-29 © Nadine Aisha Jassat, 2018; Chitra Ramaswamy's text pp38-40 © Chitra Ramaswamy, 2018;

All rights reserved

Editor: Nicola Edwards
Design: Rocket Design (East Anglia) Ltd
Artwork by Oli Frape
ISBN 978 1 5263 0399 8
10 9 8 7 6 5 4 3 2 1

MIX
Paper from
responsible sources
FSC
www.fsc.org   FSC® C104740

LONDON BOROUGH OF SUTTON
LIBRARY SERVICE

30119 028 740 38 1	
Askews & Holts	07-Oct-2020
J305.8	

Wayland, an imprint of
Hachette Children's Group
Part of Hodder and Stoughton
Carmelite House
50 Victoria Embankment
London EC4Y 0DZ

An Hachette UK Company
www.hachette.co.uk
www.hachettechildrens.co.uk

Printed and bound in Dubai

We would like to thank Media Diversified and Bare Lit Fest for championing writers of colour.

Picture acknowledgements:
Back cover (left) Claire Heuchan, (right) Ailsa Fineron; p5 Elsa Dorfman/Wikimedia Commons; p7 Shutterstock.com; p8 Claire Heuchan; p10 Ailsa Fineron; p13 Wikimedia Commons; p14 Richard Harris; p15 NBC-TV/Kobal/REX/Shutterstock; p16 TopFoto.co.uk; p17 National Archives via Wikimedia Commons; p18 Henry Nicholls; p19 Wikimedia Commons; p21 Getty Images (Handout); p22 Alamy (Jamie Mann / Alamy Stock Photo); p23 UKTV's Dave; p24 Shutterstock.com; p25 Shutterstock.com; p27 Alamy; p28 Liz Wawrykow; p30 Becky Olaniyi; p31 Shutterstock.com; p32 Everett Collection Inc /Alamy Stock Photo; p33 (all) Shutterstock.com; p34 James Barlow; p37 Shutterstock.com; p38 Claire Black; p39 Wikimedia Commons; p40 (t) Ailsa Fineron, (b) Shutterstock.com; p41 Claire Heuchan; p43 Shutterstock.com; p45 Getty Images (David M Benett / Contributor)

Every attempt has been made to clear copyright. Should there be any inadvertent omission, please apply to the publisher for rectification.

The website addresses (URLs) included in this book were valid at the time of going to press. However, it is possible that contents or addresses may have changed since the publication of this book. No responsibility for any such changes can be accepted by either the author or the Publisher.

CONTENTS

WHAT IS RACE?

Despite all the baggage that gets attached to it, race in itself is actually quite simple. A race is a group of people who share the same ancestry, and can be identified by shared physical traits like the colour of their skin and the texture of their hair. Some people think of race as scientific fact, and other people see it as a kind of social identity that is used to give meaning to shared identity and culture. Either way, race has become a significant type of category – something very much worth exploring.

Given that race and skin colour are so clearly visible to the eye, it is strange that the subject of racism gets covered up and made invisible so regularly. Talking about race is often tricky. From a very young age, many of us are fed a message that speaking about race is a racist thing to do. We are taught that simply acknowledging people's ethnic backgrounds – and the differences between those backgrounds – is a form of racism. This isn't true. Talking about race is not automatically racist.

Talking about race

What makes it even more confusing is that while talking about race gets frowned upon for being racist, it's pretty typical for racist words and actions to be passed off as harmless. For example, a white woman touches a black woman's hair when she hasn't asked permission. People claiming this isn't racist might describe it as a compliment or simple appreciation, but they don't say much about how treating black women like animals in a petting zoo is inappropriate or why overlooking a black woman's consent is harmful.

Where do you come from, originally?

And then there is the classic question: 'Where do you come from, originally?' People who claim that this question isn't racist might say they're just being curious, they have a passion for family history, or there's no harm in asking. However, the fact that this is often a sequence of questions (e.g. 'Where are you from? Where are you really from? And where are your parents from?') put together by a stranger who doesn't know you well enough to be aware of any answer proves one thing: what they're really asking is 'If you're not white, why are you here?'

Discussing difference

Difference isn't the problem. How people approach difference often is – especially when that difference has got something to do with race. Race can be a bit of a sore point with some people – especially white people – who are afraid of where talking about it will lead. They have an underlying worry: 'What if I get called racist?' That unease shapes many discussions about race. So bringing up race in a conversation isn't always straightforward, because race is treated like something that's too delicate to handle or too dangerous to approach.

Sharing experiences

This book aims to cut through the tension surrounding race to answer questions about why it matters. It explains what racism is and why racism exists in the first place. There are 'Think Abouts' to help you understand how racism works and what we can do to challenge it. People of colour will share their experiences of race in the hope of encouraging you to combat racism (when it's safe) and celebrate difference. Some of their experiences involve being targeted by racist language, but it's impossible to get to the root of the issues caused by racism without looking at how language is used as a weapon. Though it's not always easy, being able to explore race is essential.

> "It is not our differences that divide us. It is our inability to recognise, accept and celebrate those differences."
>
> **Audre Lorde, activist and writer**

WHO ARE RACISTS?

People don't always react well to being told about their own racism. They can feel guilty about having said or done something wrong, and embarrassed about having it pointed out. This can result in the person who showed racism getting defensive instead of being open to thinking about why their behaviour was racist and how they can change it. People take being identified as racist very personally, and so don't always think about the politics of racism – that it's a system their actions are part of.

Even when people are aware of racism, they can hesitate to point it out because of the implication that somebody has been racist. In a weird way, people – especially white people – can be more offended by someone being called racist than the existence of racism in itself. So we end up in a strange situation where there is racism but, supposedly, no racists. Except racism is produced by people who are racist – so if we are ever to pull apart the racist structures of our society, there must be a way to say who is propping them up.

A strange situation

Some of the confusion over what racism is comes from the ways it is obscured and excused. This is partly because identifying racism can be a bit awkward for the person who has said or done something racist – typically a white person. There comes an idea that we can't call racism by its name in case feelings are hurt. But racism needs to be brought up because feelings have already been hurt – experiencing racism is painful for people of colour. And, more than being painful, racism keeps people of colour at a social disadvantage.

Prejudice, power and privilege

Racism is about prejudice and power. If a white person discriminates against a person of colour, they are prejudiced and – what makes the difference – hold the social power in that exchange.

Being white comes with a level of privilege. That doesn't mean white people never experience problems or face struggles. But white people are not harmed by or because of how people think of whiteness. White people do not worry about being rejected from a job or denied a place to live because of the colour of their skin. White people do not worry that they will be wrongly accused of a crime because of the colour of their skin. White people do not worry that the colour of their skin closes doors for them and do not always realise that the colour of their skin in fact opens doors for them – that is white privilege.

No amount of wealth, fame, or status can completely shelter a person of colour from racism. Ignoring racism doesn't make it go away, though it might feel like the easier option. But if we cannot talk about racism, we cannot identify it. If we cannot identify racism, we cannot challenge it. If we cannot challenge racism, nothing about our lives or the society we live in will ever change for the better.

When he was elected President of the United States, Barack Obama became one of the most powerful men in the world. But he still experienced racist abuse and death threats due to attitudes towards his skin colour and Kenyan heritage. Donald Trump, who became president after Obama, even demanded to see his birth certificate because he refused to believe Obama was American.

THINK ABOUT

Have you or has someone you know experienced racism?

Claire Heuchan

Claire Heuchan is an author and award-winning feminist blogger. She spends too much time on the internet arguing against inequality (and looking at pictures of baby animals).

I grew up black, which is pretty normal – millions and millions of people around the planet do. What's less typical is that I grew up as the only black person in an otherwise white family. In many ways I was very lucky as a child, because I was always surrounded by love. I have so many good memories of being a kid: my mum taking me on weekly adventures to the library, going to the swimming pool with my grandparents on holiday, getting my first pet (a sweet, chubby hamster called Rose). But it was lonely, being a different colour from all of my family and most of my friends. Their experiences were different from mine in hundreds of small ways, and quite a few bigger ones.

There were a lot of things that my family, even though they loved me very much, couldn't protect me from. As a kid I understood that there were these awkward, painful moments that happened to me but not to white children – I knew those moments had something to do with the colour of my skin and the texture of my hair.

Every so often, an adult would ask where I was from originally. Even though I've lived in Scotland since I was born, they couldn't have been more surprised if I'd said: 'You've caught me – planet Mars is where I'm really from.' Nobody was every curious about where my mum came from, never mind where she lived 'before here'. I dreaded these moments, and my stomach twisted into knots when I felt that question coming.

'So ... Where are you from?' a friend of the family asks me.

'Near Glasgow,' I say. 'I travelled here with my grandparents.'

'No, I mean – where do you live?'

I name the small Scottish town where I have lived since birth, with said grandparents, and point them out. This short biography isn't enough.

'But …' He frowns. He presses a pale finger against my wrist and points. 'How on earth did you get that, then?'

There's nothing there. No dirt or bruises. Just my wrist, brown and a little bit boney, same as always. And I realise: the blemish he's pointing at is my skin.

Security guards were also interested in me, even though the rest of my family escaped their notice: they stopped me in airports when everyone else went on ahead. My family would linger, waiting for a stranger to finish patting down my body, and shame clouded over my excitement about the holiday.

I'd fold into myself as hairdressers argued over who had to cut my hair, telling me that I'd look a lot prettier if it was straight. Learning that a group of parents called me 'that cheery coloured girl' came as a shock – plenty of worse names were used in the playground, but somehow I'd thought adults would know better. If I live to be one hundred, I'll never forget the deep humiliation of a boy telling me my brown skin was the exact same colour as poo.

As a kid I never challenged behaviour I now know is racist. It made me anxious in ways I didn't know how to put into words without that volatile mix of anger and sadness leaking out. There was an idea that I had to be on best behaviour, because if I misbehaved then people would think all black children were naughty. Even then I knew that none of the white children were expected to act like little ambassadors for all white people – they were just allowed to be themselves, which meant being naughty sometimes.

My family didn't know how to explain racism to me. I think, like a lot of white people, they didn't give much thought to racism because it didn't do them any harm. And I didn't have the language to explain something they had never experienced. No matter how close we were, it felt like I was living in one world and they were living in another.

"As a kid I understood that there were these awkward, painful moments that happened to me but not to white children."

MY EXPERIENCE

Nikesh Shukla writes fiction, essays and for television as well as a weekly column for the *Observer*. On top of writing books, he has co-founded *The Good Journal*, a magazine written by people of colour, and The Good Literary Agency, an organisation aiming to improve representation in publishing.

I'm seventeen years old and I'm cycling to the shops. I cycle up the high street to the pedestrian crossing. Seeing the roads clear, I cycle out on to the road.

A car hits my bike and I fall to the ground.

The car screeches to a halt and the driver gets out to assess the damage. Bystanders run over to me to see if I'm okay. I'm fine. Bruised. Scared. I manage to get to my feet, with the help of a passer-by.

'Didn't you see me, you blind paki?' the woman says, inspecting the front of her car, ensuring there's been no damage.

'Watch where you're going next time. I might not stop.'

She gets back into her car and drives away at great speed.

I walk my bike home. The wheel is bent and it's unrideable. It takes me an hour to do the ten-minute journey. I'm shaking. I'm cold.

I cannot sleep.

Those words come back to me.

Blind paki.

I never heard them said before as an insult. Not in real life. Not aggressively.

Blind paki.

The word means something different from when me and my cousins use it on each other. When we say it, for some reason it's harmless and funny. It now no longer feels harmless and funny.

I start to feel like a 'paki'. My body begins to reject everything it considers 'paki'-like. Bhangra clatters cheesily in my ears, making me cringe. Bollywood films become too long and too melodramatic. Gujarati words have the same rhythm as bud-bud-ding-ding.

I have saved up money to buy a new bike. Dad offers to take me shopping. I decline. Getting back on a bike feels impossible.

I decline invitations to go out, to go to the cinema, to go bowling, to go check out the record shops in the town centre.

I start coming up with excuses to call Mum from the school payphone, just so I can confirm what time she's going to pick me up. If I have to wait for more than ten minutes for her to arrive, I get cold sweats. Friends take the train but it feels too exposed to me.

I eventually find a Saturday job, and it helps. I start to spread my wings. I start to take buses and trains by myself again. I feel confident walking the streets without my mum and dad picking me up. One day I'm on tills.

A man approaches the counter and looks up at me. Seeing me, he steps out of the queue.

'Are you okay?' I ask. 'Can I help you, sir?'

He shakes his head. 'I'll wait for her,' he says.

'I can help you sir,' I tell him.

'No,' he says firmly. 'I would prefer someone who speaks English.'

Not realising the implication he's making, I persist, naively.

'I speak English, sir. I was born here,' I say.

I smile.

'That does not make you f-ing English,' he says.

He puts the Gameboy games down on the counter next to me and he leaves the shop, shaking his head.

Years later I'm standing in line to see the late night set at a comedy club with my friend.

I step out of the queue for a second. When I step back in, I hear someone whisper to her boyfriend behind me.

'Check out this paki, pushing in.'

'What did you call me?' I ask, loudly.

'Excuse me?' she says.

She is immediately defensive, her hands crossing in front of her chest.

Her boyfriend leans towards me.

'Bruv,' he says, with faux congeniality. 'I don't know what you think you heard.'

'You called me a paki,' I say, ignoring him. 'I heard you.'

She sighs.

Years later, I hear it again when a nameless troll on Twitter, threatens to set me on fire because our political views differ. When I complain about this in a group of my friends later, someone tells me to not worry, it's just one idiot. This is just an isolated incident, he reassures me. It'll all settle down.

I look at my friend, quietly, and realise that he does not understand that one simple word, used in this way, can change someone's life. And not in a good way.

"… one simple word, used in this way, can change someone's life."

WHY DOES **SKIN COLOUR** MATTER?

In a perfect world, maybe, you could argue that skin colour doesn't matter. But in this one, it does. It's important we celebrate the things that make us different as much as we do the things that make us the same. So as things stand, skin colour matters.

From the extreme to the everyday

Racism operates on a scale. On one end, you have the horrible stuff: people killing unarmed black teenagers because they're 'scared', lynchings, slavery, white supremacy. And on the other end, you have the more everyday stuff. Where what people say and do is still racist, even if they'd consider themselves not to be.

In these cases, these everyday instances of racism are passed off as jokes, comments, nothing too serious. But they are serious, because they still add to the feeling that being different is a problem, being not white is not normal and that there are still negative associations with different skin colours.

What counts as 'normal'?

For example, someone might say, 'I'm not racist. I don't see skin colour'. Which seems silly. Because we do see it. What that person means is, 'I am choosing to not treat you as a stereotype relating to your skin colour. I am choosing to treat you as normal'. Which is great, until we start to look at what counts as normal, or universal, or default, or even the standard.

So skin colour matters because of this idea of what counts as normal. Acknowledging people's skin colour and the differences between us as individuals and people from different backgrounds allows us to see that there perhaps isn't such a clearcut thing as 'normal.'

"I remember very clearly a warm autumn day, sitting ... with my school friends aged fourteen. One girl looked at me, a slight tone of pity in her voice, and said 'Don't worry, Af, we don't see you as black'. The others concurred.

I remember their faces; kind, accommodating, distancing themselves proudly from any possibility that they could be accused of being racist, and at the same time willing to overlook the problem my very existence created.

This act of kindness is one of the most traumatic things that has ever happened to me. It taught me that being black is bad."

Afua Hirsch, writer and broadcaster

Influenced by immigration

Sure, once Britain was a white nation built from influences ranging from many different places. For many centuries, this country has been host to immigrants from many lands. The Celts were followed by the Romans, by the Angles, then the Jutes, Saxons, Danes, Norwegians, Normans, Bretons and French. Then we had the British Empire, and due to things like slavery and trade, we had a lot more movement of people around the world. And with an influx of immigrants from the Caribbean, South Asia and certain countries in Africa, we have the wonderful, racially rich and multicultural country we enjoy today.

This is a country built by and for many people, and our differences are just as important as our similarities. Which is why skin colour does matter.

Britain's love of curry can be traced to the first restaurant in the nation to serve it: the Hindoostane Coffee House in London which was opened in 1810 by a Muslim soldier, Sake Dean Mahomed.

MY EXPERIENCE

Derek Owusu is a host of the book podcast *Mostly Lit*, which was voted one of iTunes' Best Podcasts and BBC Culture's Top 25 Podcasts That Will Blow Your Mind. He's working on a book of essays by and for black British men with the goal of inspiring and educating people.

I must have stood out like a sore thumb growing up. As a child, I lived in Long Melford, Suffolk, one of many foster children in an all-white household and village. No one ever mentioned it. No one acknowledged my skin colour, ever. Behind the British politeness and each faked smile I knew there was the seemingly open-minded thought of, 'I don't see you as black; you're just like everybody else.' But unfortunately in Suffolk, that 'everybody' was white. And I wasn't.

In school, my best friend Stephen – Stevie for short – was my sparring partner. He laughed and coughed like an old man with bronchitis any time I'd give him a blow on the back. He never cried, though, and always laughed his way through whatever pain I inflicted. I, on the other hand, cried all the time. Stevie was stronger than I was, and he knew it. I was like a toy he could break, test his strength on, and feel no

remorse about. After a rough fight he'd come into school the next day and show me the marks I'd left on him. I was proud of this – because even though he'd always get the better of me, no trace of our fights could be found on my body.

But after a while, the bruises on Stevie took on a different meaning. He became an adventurer, a fighter who had been through it all and survived. Other kids looked at his skin and were impressed with rough circles of purple. I became jealous. And so I allowed Stevie to land more punches than he'd usually be capable of. The pain would be worth it, because the next day I could show off my battle scars, too.

It didn't happen. No matter how hard I was hit, nothing showed up on my skin. Confused, I looked at my arms the morning after a beating and wondered what was wrong. Soon after, I stopped fighting with Stevie and instead watched on from a playground bench as the other kids bonded through battle. This feeling, one of difference and isolation, stayed with me.

Then something happened that made my bubble a bit more bearable.

I remember the first time I saw him on TV. His afro hair was shaven into a controlled single line, so dark you couldn't see the curls but could imagine their softness; his large black arms were so tightly smooth that you thought the muscles beneath the skin were about to tear through. Gold chains were splashed about his neck without weighing him down; he stood tall, with his head held high. Who I was – everything I was – suddenly made sense when I first saw Mr T: because I was him. A younger him, but I had this tough dark-skinned man to look forward to becoming when I grew up.

Mr T from the TV show The A-Team.

I didn't care that I couldn't bruise – my potential body was too strong. And looking at his hair, I knew I could make mine the same while none of my school friends could; I knew then that there were different kinds of people in the world – some who bruised and others who didn't. Mr T and I were the type who didn't. Yeah, we were a different kind of person. And for the first time, difference meant more to me than sameness.

The next day, when I walked into school, I was ready to fight. I could take on the world. Nobody could stop Mr T.

> **"... for the first time, difference meant more to me than sameness."**

RACE AND **RACISM** IN HISTORY

Britain has a long and complicated history with race. There's a popular belief that people of colour have only been part of life in Britain during recent history, that before the last two hundred years happened, only white people lived in the United Kingdom.

An incorrect assumption

This belief is created by all-white casts in historical films, the way we are taught history in schools, and an assumption that to be British is to be white. But the belief that Britain was a strictly white country until the Windrush generation began migrating to Britain after the Second World War is wrong. It's wrong because it's factually incorrect, and it's wrong because excluding people of colour from British identity is racist.

People of colour have lived on these islands for thousands of years. We have been a part of Britain since before the Romans set foot on British soil, since before the birth of Jesus Christ. But sometimes certain people like to dream of a Britain that never was; a Britain

Passengers from Jamaica arrive in Britain on the Empire Windrush in 1948.

in which everyone is white. An early example of someone who dreamed of this was Queen Elizabeth I, who reigned from 1558 to 1603. Five hundred years ago, she tried to have the Mayor of London pass a law demanding that all black people leave the country because, she said, there were 'already here to manie'. Her attempt failed.

An empire built on exploitation

Although Elizabeth wanted to keep the nation as white as possible, it was during her reign that Britain began creating an empire that would reach around the world. British merchants became rich from entering the slave trade, buying and selling African people like objects. British merchants built huge wealth from sugar, tobacco and rum – products made with slave labour.

Writing people of colour out of British history hides some of the strongest sources of racial tension. The British Empire grew from violently exploiting people of colour. It created outposts across the world – including Gibraltar, Bermuda, and different Caribbean Islands – where British officers held authority over native peoples and took precious natural resources from their land for the profit of the Empire. Slavery and colonialism also brought more people of colour on to British soil, having connected us to the Empire.

Against immigration

Fast-forward to recent history and British politicians are making speeches about people of colour and immigrants that claim we are a threat to British society. During his infamous 'Rivers of Blood'

The Westminster Tournament Roll of 1511 shows John Blanke, a 'blacke trumpeter' in the courts of Henry VII and Henry VIII.

speech given in 1968, Conservative MP Enoch Powell claimed that an increase in the number of people of colour migrating to Britain would result in terrible violence. Nigel Farage, former leader of UKIP, played on these fears in the run-up to Britain's vote to leave the European Union in 2016. His politics were anti-immigration, the language and style of his campaign using a stealthy type of racism.

Being selective in what we remember about Britain's history makes it impossible to fully understand how the problems of today – like racism – came to be.

"Every black person's life, no matter what it is, is part of the black experience. Because being black in a white country comes with ... complications and contradictions."

Andrea Levy, writer

Inua Ellams

Inua Ellams is a poet, playwright and performer. He has published four books of poetry and his first play *Barber Shop Chronicles*, had two sold-out runs at England's National Theatre in London. His work covers themes of identity, destiny, race and place.

Can we have some toast please?

So, February was my girlfriend's birthday. I thought, to celebrate, let's escape the urban jungle of London! Let's go to a real one! Okay, maybe a small forest, with a nice hotel in the middle. I looked online and actually found one!

When I called them, really excitedly, to book a room, they advised me to book a table for dinner as well because it would get really busy. The restaurant looked really nice and posh in the pictures so I agreed, but when we arrived, the manager pointed to what looked like a school canteen and told us we would be eating there. This wasn't what I paid £78 for!

It was so cold and noisy there that night that my girlfriend and I had to wear scarves and shout to have a conversation. But the hotel's restaurant next door, the one I saw in the pictures was warm and quiet, so I asked the managers if we could eat there instead, but he said they were fully booked ... no space for us. We had to stay in the canteen, but every time we got up to use the toilet, we looked into the nice restaurant, and every time we looked, there were at least ten free tables ... so we wondered why he said they were full.

The next morning, we went for breakfast. A white couple were behind us in the queue. We sat down, gave our orders and waited patiently for the food, but it took a really long time to come. The white couple who were behind us, who gave their breakfast orders after us, somehow got their meals before we did. They were half-way through before ours arrived! We also had to ask three times before our teas and apple juice came, and then we asked for toast.

When the toast came, only two small, half-burnt slices arrived, on a cold plate. Everyone else, who just happened to be

> "... this is one of the things living in a country that has a history of racism does ... it makes you question everything."

white, got lovely small baskets of warm bread. We asked for more toast and this time, it was half-warm and practically soggy. We tried one more time 'Can we have some toast, please? Actually toasted?' and the waiter just grunted at us! He was serving a table full of white women next to us, saying things like 'Enjoy your meal madam!' and smiling as he spoke, and all we got was grunts!

The waiter even got my girlfriend's breakfast wrong. When we told them, the waiter just grabbed her plate, returned ten minutes later, dropped it on the table, and left! He didn't even say 'Sorry we got your food wrong' or anything!

My girlfriend is of Vietnamese ethnic origins and I am of Nigerian ethnic origins. That night, instead of relaxing and enjoying our holiday, we were wondering if they treated us like that because we weren't white. We don't know for sure – we will never know, only they know why – but this is one of the things that living in a country that has a history of racism does ... it makes you question everything.

It is like visiting a house that used to be haunted and everyone telling you 'All the ghosts are gone! It is perfectly safe now!' Even if it is true, every time you hear a door slam, steps creak or feel a cold breeze, you wonder 'Are there still ghosts? Are they out to get me? Am I in danger?' Now, imagine having to stay in that haunted house for ten minutes. For one week. For one year. For your whole life.

THINK ABOUT

How do you think the way history is told shapes a person's sense of belonging in Britain? And in what way do you think race shapes this experience?

SO, HOW FAR HAVE WE COME?

In 1968, Mahesh Upadhyaya, an engineer living in Huddersfield, West Yorkshire, tried to buy a house. The building company responsible for the estate told him that they had a company policy to not sell houses to coloured people, lest they bring the value of the area down. Mahesh told them that this was now illegal, because the Race Relations Act came into being in 1968. Mahesh Upadhyaya took this building company to court and was the first person to bring a case of racial discrimination under the Race Relations Act in the whole of the UK. The case was lost on a technicality, but the judge said that, technicality aside, discrimination had taken place. The building company changed its policy and this was a small victory for a man who risked everything to stand up for what he believed in. Mahesh is author Nikesh's uncle.

Nikesh and his uncle sometimes talk about how far we've come and what has changed. In 2017, a landlord called Fergus Wilson was found to be prohibiting Indian and Pakistani families from renting properties from him because of what he described in a leaked email as 'the curry smell'. This was found unlawful by a court. So between 1968 and 2017, with two cases that sound so familiar, how much has changed?

HATE ON THE RISE

In June 2015, in a church in Charleston, South Carolina, USA, Dylann Roof, a white supremacist, killed nine African-American churchgoers.

In the UK, in 2016, after the Brexit referendum, there was a 46 per cent rise in hate crimes. A 2015 *Sun* newspaper column in which Katie Hopkins described migrants as 'cockroaches' and 'feral humans' resembled pro-genocide propaganda, the United Nations High Commissioner for Human Rights, Zeid Ra'ad Al Hussein, said.

In August 2017, in Charlottesville, Virginia, USA, a protest against a rally held by white supremacists, which resulted in the death of a protestor, showed that there was the resurgence of white supremacists in America, emboldened by a president who said that there were good and bad people on both sides of the debate.

THE MURDER OF
STEPHEN LAWRENCE

Stephen Lawrence was a young black British man from South East London with a bright future ahead of him, who was murdered in a racist attack. He was nineteen years old. His death is one of the most notorious racist murders in the history of the UK. It was a tragic loss of life and the fallout from the investigation by the police revealed that there were still profoundly racist attitudes in British society, from the grassroots level all the way up to institutions like the police investigating the murder.

Stephen was murdered in April 1993. It was only in 2012 that two of the murderers were finally convicted.

At the time of his death Stephen was studying technology and physics at the Blackheath Bluecoat School and English language and literature at Woolwich College, and was hoping to become an architect.

He and his friend Duwayne Brooks were heading home from an uncle's house when they were set upon by five men. Stephen was called the n-word before being stabbed twice. He bled to death.

After the first investigation into his murder, five men were arrested but not convicted. According to Duwayne's eyewitness account, the murder was due to racism and Stephen was killed because he was black.

The case was mishandled by the police and the Crown Prosecution Service and as a result none of the men were found guilty. There was a public inquiry into the case in 1998 by Sir William Macpherson. He was to look at the original Metropolitan Police Service (MPS) investigation. His conclusions were damning: the police force was institutionally racist. The report also detailed where the police had been ignorant, lazy, wrong or negligent in the way they investigated the case. Imagine: an officer didn't apply first aid to Stephen on arriving at the scene.

The publication in 1999 of the resulting Macpherson Report has been called 'one of the most important moments in the modern history of criminal justice in Britain'.

On 18 May 2011, it was announced that two of the original suspects, Gary Dobson and David Norris, were to stand trial for the murder in the light of 'new and substantial evidence' due to a review conducted in secret.

On 3 January 2012, Dobson and Norris were found guilty of Lawrence's murder; the pair were juveniles at the time of the crime and were sentenced to detention at Her Majesty's pleasure, equivalent to a life sentence for an adult, with minimum terms of 15 years 2 months and 14 years 3 months respectively for what the judge described as a 'terrible and evil crime'.

It's important to think about what people could have done and who they could have been. Stephen had a bright future ahead of him. And it was cut short by five men who wanted to kill him solely because he was black.

Stephen did not die in vain because his death exposed the institutional racism at the core of Britain's legal system. But, imagine a world where he was still with us today.

These newspaper front pages brought the news that Dobson and Norris had been found guilty of Stephen Lawrence's murder, almost twenty years after they had killed him.

Asim Chaudhry is an award-winning actor and writer. He is best known for co-creating the popular TV show *People Just Do Nothing*, which started life as a series of YouTube videos that went viral

Just a headache

It was the summer of '98. I was 11 years old. The World Cup was on and I was at my local park in Feltham, West London, playing football in my new football boots with my best friend, Asad. Before I share this experience let me give you some context about what football meant to us when we were kids.

It was our life!

In the morning on the way to school we would kick the ball to each other, at times it would go on the road and we would get shouted and beeped at by angry morning commuters.

At school I would stare at the clock, waiting for lunchtime, choreographing the perfect goal, doing the commentary in my head and everything!

'It's a perfect cross from the left wing whipped in by Asad Khan, Asim Chaudhry brings it down expertly with his chest, he flips it over the defender with a gravity-defying move, the goalkeeper rushes out and Asim lobs him with a bicycle kick – this is the greatest goal of all time!! Take a bow son!'

The bell for lunch would snap me out of my footballing daydream. I would sprint to the back field to have a quick five-a-side. I would try to emulate Ronaldo – not that one – the REAL one! I tried to do step-overs and take elaborate long-distance free kicks with the outside of my boot like Roberto Carlos would. The ball would rocket 100 miles into the sky! I didn't care, it was the theatre of it all that gave me the pleasure.

We would come back from lunch, covered in mud with ripped trousers. After school we would head straight to the park and do it all again, then go home and watch it on TV; we were CONSUMED by it!

When I was playing football nothing seemed to matter, not my parents' imminent divorce, my cousin's battle with cancer, the racist kids around my area who would chase me home, nothing. It was pure escapism.

My dad worked as a mini cab driver and I would bug him about these new Nike Ronaldo boots that I wanted. I promised to do extra chores and even clean his car every weekend. Then one day he told me he worked all night, saved up some money and then presented me with football boots. I. WENT. WILD. I started running around the living room in a state of pure euphoria.

So back to my experience. I was with Asad in the park, wearing my new boots. Asad had just bought a brand new official France '98 World Cup football and we were practising penalties. I heard a voice, 'Let me have a shot mate.' It was the racist kids from my area; they were holding golf clubs. We ignored them. The main one said 'Oi Mowgli, I'm talking to you, don't mug me off, just one shot'. Asad gave me a look like 'maybe they'll leave us alone if we comply', and he passed them the ball. 'Thank you, come again' the main one said in an 'Apu from the Simpsons voice'. He faked a shot, then picked up the ball and started walking away. 'Come on man, he just bought that,' I said in a rather

Ronaldo of Brazil, also known as 'O Fenômeno' (The Phenomenon). At the 1998 FIFA World Cup he was awarded the Golden Ball as the tournament's best player.

meek tone. Asad gave me another look, this time it was more of a 'please shut up Asim, let them have it' type of look. These boys were much bigger and older than us. The main one with the ball came up to me and said 'You want your f-ing ball back you paki? ... here.' He kicked the ball square in my face and then punched me in the head. My face felt warm, I fell over, all I could hear was laughter. I felt my nose, blood, warm blood. Asad ran over to me, the boys left, with the ball.

We went to the shop and got someone to buy me paracetamol. I remember I had a headache, it was painful. I put two paracetamol into my coke and drank it as I was always afraid of choking when taking it the normal way, pathetic I know. My head felt heavy but I also felt something else. It was shame. We just got robbed and attacked and there was nothing we could do about it. The lack of power left shame, not 'pathetic, can't even take paracetamol' type of shame, this was real, crippling shame. I wiped away my blood and didn't tell anyone about what had happened. I've been called a paki before as I lived in a very racist area but this was the first time I was attacked right after being called one. The punishment for being brown felt so much more instant and real! My heart was racing and my head was still pounding.

I went home and didn't really want to watch the football, I still had a headache. I put my Ronaldo boots in my cupboard.

The next morning I told my mum I couldn't go to school because I had a headache. She checked my temperature and told me to stop messing about and get ready for school. I started crying and begged her to let me have the day off, 'Please mum, my head.' Knowing it was something else, my mum asked me what was wrong. I wanted to tell her but I couldn't, the shame crippled me. 'Nothing,' I said. 'Just a headache.'

"We just got robbed and attacked and there was nothing we could do about it. The lack of power left shame ... real, crippling shame."

OFFICIAL MATCH BALL OF THE FIFA WORLD CUP 1998

SKIN COLOUR AND STEREOTYPES

We're all familiar with stereotypes, like the idea that pink is for girls and blue is for boys – the best-known gender stereotype. Stereotypes are a way of reinforcing difference: they create distance between people, making racial difference into an unbridgeable gap instead of a subject that can be talked about openly. Stereotypes can be downplayed as a harmless joke, but they can actually do a lot of damage. They shape how people are viewed and understood by others, in some cases preventing the groups of people from being seen as worthy of kindness or care.

Damage and discrimination

Stereotypes are so deeply embedded into our social norms that it's not always obvious when they're having an effect. The stories we are told to help us understand the world – especially differences between people – can be rooted in stereotype.

For example, anger and violence get projected onto black boys because they are stereotyped as thugs. And, while it is an idea that gets played up for laughs or drama on television, the thug stereotype has real, severe consequences for black boys. It shapes how they are treated in lots of different places by lots of different (but mostly white) people. Black boys are three times more likely to be excluded from school than white children and significantly more likely to be charged with a crime. There is a clear connection between how black boys are stereotyped as thugs and how they are discriminated against: treated like

> **"The single story creates stereotypes, and the problem with stereotypes is not that they are untrue, but that they are incomplete. They make one story become the only story. The consequence of the single story is this: it robs people of dignity. It makes our recognition of our equal humanity difficult. It emphasises how we are different rather than how we are similar."**
>
> ### Chimamanda Ngozi Adichie, writer

threats instead of as children.

Police brutality

In 2017, fifteen-year-old Terrell Decosta Jones-Burton was beaten while being detained by the London police. He was left with missing teeth, a broken jawbone and bruising on his brain. As Theresa May said in her first speech as British Prime Minister: "If you're black, you're treated more harshly by the criminal justice system than if you're white." Though it is shocking, the violence Terrell Decosta Jones-Burton faced is part of a pattern of police brutality against black people in Britain.

Justifying racism

Whether or not we mean it, stereotypes are used to make groups of people seem less sympathetic, less worthy of respect, less human. Stereotypes are used to dehumanise people of colour. As a result, stereotypes can be used as a way to justify racism. Though it involved a lot of violence against Indian people and the theft of precious resources, Britain colonising India is still justified with the idea that Britain was a 'civilising' force. The logic of racism tells us that if white British rule was civilising, Indian people must have been uncivilised – one of the oldest racist stereotypes there is.

An example of how the British justified their presence in India as a 'civilising' influence: an English dignitary dominates an Indian procession in the 1750s.

THINK ABOUT

Can you think of any stereotypes about white people? If so, what are they? If not, can you think why that might be?

Wei Ming Kam is the co-founder of BAME In Publishing, a network for people of colour who work in publishing. As well as being a writer, she works to improve representation and support people of colour telling our own stories.

We're sitting down for dinner with the news playing on the TV. There's a short piece on civil partnerships for couples who are the same gender. Mum tuts, and I tense up. I am in my teens, and arguing with my parents is a regular occurrence.

Mum says that gay people are asking for too much now. I snap back that they just want equal rights. Dad says something about how they don't hate gay people, but he doesn't understand why they have to make such a fuss all the time. I stop arguing, knowing that it's pointless.

A few months later, at the start of sixth form, there are a few new girls in our year. One of them ends up sitting next to me in English class. She is clever and funny and sweet, and I want to be around her all the time in a way that confuses me. I realise, months later, that I have a crush on her.

What I remember the most – after the longing, and terror of being found out – is my surprise. The dinner-table arguments, my anger at my parents for not understanding why equal rights for queer people was needed, all came, I thought, from being a good straight ally. I couldn't imagine for one second that perhaps it was because I was queer myself.

The surprise stays with me for the rest of my time in school, and I swing between denying to myself that I could be attracted to girls, and bafflement that this is happening to me. I begin to notice that on every bit of news I see about queer rights, nearly everyone who is interviewed is white, and usually a man. I start looking out for TV shows to watch with characters who aren't straight, and almost without fail, they are all white. In the few books I read which have gay characters, they are white. Queer people of colour seem to just not exist.

When I go to university, the LGBT Society is mostly populated by white people. The idea of joining it does not even cross my mind.

I am searching for something that will tell me I'm not alone, and perfectly normal, and that if I'm not ok now, then I will be in future. There is nothing that reassures me about any of this, and it doesn't help me with fighting the feeling that there is something wrong with me, despite knowing, at the same time, that this isn't true.

There is a day, a few months after I graduate, when I find *Ash* in my local bookshop by an author called Malinda Lo. I've never seen a children's book by someone with a Chinese name before. When I flick through it and find out that it's a fantasy with a queer romance between two girls, my heart starts hammering. I read it in one breathless afternoon; it makes me feel less alone.

A few years later, we are celebrating my cousin's birthday and talking about our parents.

'Mum and Dad have mellowed a lot. Every time we talk about politics we still have a huge fight though. I mean, they only relaxed their views on gay rights because of me,' I say.

'I think that's just a Chinese thing, isn't it?' one of my other cousins says, shrugging. She says this as if it's a statement of fact.

I blink in surprise at what she's implying. I want to point out that homophobia is built into society, and that to believe that it is an inherently Chinese prejudice is ridiculous, and racist. There are so many stories about homophobia that involve bigoted white people, after all.

The conversation moves on before I can say anything.

Later, I wonder if my cousin was surprised when my siblings told them I had come out to my family. I think about the way everyone else listening to us said nothing, and who else may have accepted what she said because they believed it.

"I am searching for something that will tell me I'm not alone, and perfectly normal."

MY EXPERIENCE

Becky Olaniyi

Becky Olaniyi is an activist. She is a feminist, disability campaigner and a member of Sisters of Frida – a collective of disabled women living in Britain. Becky works to remove barriers to equality.

Our race is something that we get from our parents, just like eye colour or height. People can usually tell our race from looking at us. It's part of our biology, and this doesn't change.

There's a similar term that you may know: 'ethnicity'. Ethnicity means your cultural background, which is made up of things like the language you speak, the foods you eat and (maybe) your religion. People sharing these things are an ethnic group, which can be different from race. Ethnicity is something that can change, depending on what happens in your life. Ethnicity and race can overlap in some areas, and can be totally separate in others.

My parents, grandparents and great-grandparents are all from Nigeria, and have all lived there. So I am definitely Nigerian, and a black person. My family all speak Yoruba, eat Nigerian food and are Christians – one of the largest religions in Nigeria. I was born when my parents moved from Nigeria to England.

I grew up and now I don't speak Yoruba, don't eat Nigerian food, and don't go to church. I only ever speak English and I prefer Chinese food.

When I was growing up I did 'English' things at school and 'Nigerian' things at home. Even though there were lots of West African children in my class, we all tended to act differently in different places. Sometimes these worlds collided, especially when my mum took me to school. A lot of Nigerian lunch ladies at school were her friends. I always had to call them Aunty, even when my mum wasn't there and other students were. This was confusing for some classmates, who wondered how I could be related to almost all the lunch staff.

Over the years, the 'English things' that people do have changed a lot. When my mum came to this country in the 1980s, I don't think people even knew what a kebab was. She didn't see many faces that were like hers, and the

▲ Food from around the world

> "I know now that the things I used to be embarrassed about should be celebrated and defended instead of hidden."

few people that she did know kept to themselves. As time has gone by, people from across the world have made their mark on British culture: we have food and music from places where most of us have never been. Britishness has changed, resulting in people like me.

You could say my ethnicity is British, but there's more to it than that. Although I don't do some things that are part of Nigerian culture, I still understand Yoruba, still wear Nigerian clothes and still call EVERYBODY older than me

'Aunty' and 'Uncle'. My behaviour reflects both my family's beliefs and my Western upbringing.

When I was younger I wanted to fit in with my white classmates and thought that meant I had to hide who I was. I've realised I can get along with people and understand them without pretending to be something I'm not. I know now that the things I used to be embarrassed about should be celebrated and defended instead of hidden. I call myself 'Black British'.

THINK ABOUT

Becky is Nigerian, and a black person, and calls herself 'Black British'. How would you describe yourself? Which aspects of your background would you choose to celebrate?

RACE AND
REPRESENTATION

Representation is important. Finding stories about people who look like you – seeing yourself reflected in films, books, TV shows – matters. To be acknowledged and seen as part of your society is essential to belonging. Unfortunately, the quality and availability of positive representation is limited when it comes to race.

Erasure

White people can usually open a magazine or switch on the television without ever stopping to question whether they will find any people who look like or live like they do – and being acknowledged everywhere you look is a privilege. For people of colour, representation is not so simple. We are underrepresented and written out of stories, even stories we are part of in the real world – this is called erasure. And even when people of colour are present in stories, racism can define how we are shown. People of colour are too often reduced to the sidekick of a white main character, with no life beyond providing a white friend support, or being criminals on the wrong side of the law.

In this film still, actors reconstruct one of the doll tests carried out by Professor Phipps Clark (see page 33).

The Doll Test

There is a famous experiment called the Doll Test. It was created by two psychologists, Kenneth and Mamie Phipps Clark, to find out how racism and racial segregation shape the way black children understand themselves. Children under ten are given two dolls, one of which is black and the other is white. Most children identify the white doll as being pretty and nice. Most children identify the black doll as bad. The Doll Test is revealing, because it shows how children are taught to see positive things about pale skin and negative things about dark skin.

Self-worth and self-representation

In a subtle way, representation shapes self-worth and even what we imagine is possible in how we live our own lives. Seeing characters that look like us going on adventures, falling in love, becoming artists, travelling through space or even doing everyday things like picking up some bread at the supermarket – it's important because it gives us affirmation and inspiration.

New technology has brought new ways of creating stories, and the best part is that anyone can tell them. You don't need to work in film or television to share a story with an audience. People of colour create popular videos, podcasts, blogs, vlogs and everything in between. Through telling our own stories where we can, people of colour get more control over how our image is represented. Self-representation means that people of colour are less likely to be defined in relation to white characters, but instead appreciated as the main characters of our own stories.

> "Until I saw people who looked like me, doing the things I wanted to, I wasn't so sure it was a possibility. Seeing Whoopi Goldberg and Oprah in *The Color Purple*, it dawned on me: 'Oh — I could be an actress!' We plant the seed of possibility."
>
> **Lupita Nyong'o, actress**

◀ *Whoopi Goldberg*

▲ *Oprah Winfrey*

◀ *Lupita Nyong'o*

Nadine Aisha Jassat

Nadine Aisha Jassat is a writer and expert in challenging gender-based violence, whose work connects storytelling and social justice. She works with young people on issues to do with equality, including creative participation work with young women of colour. In 2018 she won a New Writers Award from the Scottish Book Trust.

On bangles and belonging

When I was a teenager, my Aunt gave me two gold bangles, straight from a long stack that she wore on her arm. My family are Zimbabwean-Indians, and for my Auntie, wearing gold bracelets was part of her connection to the Indian side of her heritage. When she gave me two bracelets from the string that she wore every day, it felt like she was connecting me not only to that heritage, but to her.

I grew up in the UK, and my Dad's side of the family were a long plane trip away in Zimbabwe. Often, I would get asked to explain where I was from – by other kids at school, teachers, friends and even just strangers on the street. My Mum is White British, and my Dad has African and Indian heritage, and his family have been in Zimbabwe for generations.

When people asked where I was from, sometimes they weren't satisfied with a simple answer of 'Yorkshire'; they'd push and ask 'originally, but originally'. Suddenly, 'Yorkshire' turned into a longer story, and it didn't feel like it was my choice whether or not I wanted to tell it.

It can be hard to feel like you fully belong in the place where you were born and raised when there are people seemingly queuing up to tell you otherwise. In the UK, some people pointed out that I was different, that when they saw me they saw someone 'out of place'. But then when I went to Zimbabwe, it was clear I wasn't from there, either. One of my favourite poems, *Questions for Ada* by Ijeoma Umebinyuo, captures this perfectly: 'here you are, too foreign for home, too

> **"I began to realise I could make my home based on my terms, not anyone else's."**

foreign for here, never enough for both'. That was how I felt – like I was always trying to straddle two places, two homes, and wasn't able to fully belong to either.

It wasn't easy, but I began to realise I could make my home based on my terms, not anyone else's. If home is where the heart is, then home was where my heart felt happiest and most alive; in Scotland, a country I chose for myself, and in Southern Africa, wherever my family and Southern African-Indian culture were. I realised I could belong to more than one place, and that by defining belonging on my own terms, I could transform my feeling of being straddled between two worlds, into embracing and loving all the different things from those worlds which came together in me.

Now, as an adult, I help other young people on the same journey. We talk about wearing hijabs and high-tops,

drinking Irn-Bru with a Masala Dosa. We realise that we're allowed to be who we are, and that there's something wonderful in our unique mixes. The truer we are to ourselves, the more we can lead by example, too, and help others to feel brave enough to embrace their own path.

Around eight years after my Auntie first gave me my bracelets, which I had worn every day since, they slipped off, and I thought I had lost them. I panicked – in losing my bracelets, had I lost the thing which tied a thread keeping her and my heritage with me? No; I might have lost the talisman I could look to as a reminder, but I hadn't lost the magic. The connection to my family and heritage was something I carried with me all along. I only needed to believe in it for that connection to be there: carried with me in my writing, actions and words. In who I am, always.

THINK ABOUT

Nadine describes how she belongs to more than one place. Where would you say that you belong to? How would you define who you are?

RACE AND
RIGHTS

There are legal protections in place to help you combat racism when you see it.

The Equality Act 2010 is a law that says you cannot be discriminated against because of your race.

According to the Act, race is defined as your colour, ethnic/racial group or nationality. This can be the country you were born in or the country you are a resident in. It could also mean where your ethnic origins are from. For example, you may have Indian origins but hold a British passport.

Race discrimination is when you are treated differently because of your race in a situation covered by the Equality Act. It could be a one-off incident or it could be because there is a rule or policy in place that is discriminatory. It doesn't have to be on purpose in order to be unlawful.

In terms of the law, there are four main types of race discrimination.

Direct discrimination: This is when someone treats you worse than someone else in a similar situation because of your race. For example, in 2017, landlord Fergus Wilson's rental policy of not renting to Indian and Pakistani tenants 'because of the curry smell' was found by the Equalities And Human Rights Commission to be unlawful (see page 20).

Indirect discrimination: This is when an organisation has a policy/way of working that puts people of your racial group at a disadvantage. An example of this could be where a company bans its staff from conversing in any language other than English, including personal conversations. This could result in discrimination against people who do not have English as their first language, meaning they are not able to work there.

#GHOSTBUSTERS

Leslie Jones was subjected to a barrage of racist and sexist abuse after she appeared as the only actor of colour in an all-female remake of Ghostbusters in 2016.

Harassment: This is where someone makes a person feel humiliated, offended or degraded. Actor Leslie Jones was recently the victim of a targeted slew of racist (and sexist) harassment when she took a role in the reboot of the *Ghostbusters* film. Harassment could be as obvious as using racial slurs or it could be about subtly inferring that one person's race is inferior to another's.

Victimisation: This is when someone is treated badly because they have made a complaint of race related discrimination under the Equality Act. For example, a person may make a formal complaint about some racist treatment they are receiving. A manager could then put undue pressure on that person to withdraw the complaint.

The Equality Act came in in 2010 and covers a heap of things alongside race. It was put in place to bring together lots of different acts around discrimination, including the Equal Pay Act 1970, the Sex Discrimination Act 1975, the Race Relations Act 1976, the Disability Discrimination Act 1995 and some laws around workplace discrimination to do with religion or belief, sexual orientation and age.

If you think you might have been treated unfairly and want further advice, you can contact the Equality Advisory and Support Service. The details are on page 47, along with other useful addresses and links.

Chitra Ramaswamy

Chitra Ramaswamy is a journalist, book reviewer, and feature writer. Her first book, *Expecting*, won the Saltire First Book of the Year Award 2016. She is currently working on her first novel.

An average school day. A sunny day, perhaps in the sluggish hour after lunch break, maybe in the ravenous hour before. I am 12, maybe 13: a skinny, mouthy, sensitive teenager with a ferocious love of books, despite never finding anyone with the same colour skin as me in their pages. I wouldn't even know, in fact, to look for them. It is the early 1990s in a rowdy South West London comprehensive with a playground that brims with the threat of footballs coming full tilt at your head, often purposefully aimed, and big ethnically mixed classes that might one day be celebrated for their diversity but right now are just, well, tense.

A boy in art class, a small, popular boy who is always hassling me (never would I use the word bullied, I am too ashamed to even think it), lifts his index fingers. Both pads have been carefully dipped in black paint. One represents my classmate, a serious, bespectacled British Asian boy (this is what we are told to call ourselves: British Asian or, sometimes, ethnic minority) who has the misfortune of almost sharing my surname. The other is me. He squishes his fingers, smashes the little black faces together roughly, says things that may as well be arrows firing at my chest. Words that I hear on the bus, in the street, playground, supermarket queues, round people's houses. Words that will eventually come to be referred to covertly, like swear words, by their first letters alone. Words that no matter how

> **"You are more than the colour of your skin, more than your race, more than the boxes you tick and the places you are pressed to explain you are from. "**

they are signified will never lose their power to knock me sideways.

Everyone in the class laughs. There is no escape, no teacher (in my memory anyway), no way of surviving other than to sit very still and wait for it to be over.

Summoning this memory makes it hurt all over again, which, I've learned, is typical of experiencing racism: to hurt, always. To flood your 20, 30, 39 (I'm not 40 yet!) year-old self with shame and pain, no matter how long it has been or how far you have come. How extraordinary that just a few words said by people who have long since left your life can be carried so far.

My adult self looks back on this now and can name it as an instance of racism. It didn't particularly stand out; it was merely the first one that sprung to mind as I sat down to write this. There it was, waiting for me, still hurting. And something else that escaped my notice

in those difficult years. That small, popular boy was mixed race. He had his own experiences of living in his brown skin, being treated differently. The boy with black fingers was black too.

So this is what I want to say, not to the mixed race boy with fingers blackened with paint, but to the brown-skinned daughter of south Indian immigrants sitting very still and waiting for it to be over. Racism comes in as many different forms as there are different people. The experience of your own race at any moment in time, in any culture, at any age, in any place, is never done. This is exhausting, confusing, painful, but it is also joyful. It is who you are. You are more than the colour of your skin, more than your race, more than the boxes you tick and the places you are pressed to explain you are from. You are more than this. But be proud. Keep reading. Occupy your space. Because you are also this.

THINK ABOUT

Chitra says that racism comes in as many different forms as there are different people. What different forms of racism you have seen, or heard, or experienced?

HOW DOES IT FEEL TO EXPERIENCE RACISM?

Often when I have witnessed racism or been the victim of it, I've really noticed that my feelings are very rarely taken into account. This can be a severe cause of depression and anxiety. You read my essay on pages 10-11 of this book. You know what I went through. Often, I find that racism can result in managing the feelings of the person saying the problematic thing, rather than how that racism has affected you.

If the person knows what they say is racist, the onus is thrown on to you to prove that what they said was wrong. This can prove exhausting.

And if the person didn't realise, you have to manage their defensiveness or upset because they said something wrong. This can end up distracting you or upsetting you. I find often that the best way for me to deal with these things is to very calmly explain what has happened and what effect that has had on me. I also will prioritise the effect the event has had on me over the other person. This is important. It shows you that you are prioritising yourself. It's a reminder that you are allowed to feel angry, upset, anxious, righteous and you own your feelings only, not anyone else's.

Often, people will demand to know what they can do to help you fight racism if you are a person of colour. 'How can I help you?' they will say.

My reply to them is this: 'It is not your responsibility to help me fight racism. It is your responsibility to be anti-racist in your own spaces, your community, your friendship circle, your family. I'll do the same in mine. We can only manage the environments we move in. So if you want to help, help your community. And I'll help mine.'

Nikesh Shukla

"The function, the very serious function of racism is distraction. It keeps you from doing your work. It keeps you explaining, over and over again, your reason for being. Somebody says you have no language and you spend twenty years proving that you do. Somebody says your head isn't shaped properly so you have scientists working on the fact that it is. Somebody says you have no art, so you dredge that up. Somebody says you have no kingdoms, so you dredge that up. None of this is necessary. There will always be one more thing."

Toni Morrison, writer

Experiencing racism can be traumatic. It is deeply painful, to be treated as less than human because of what you are. And it can feel desperately lonely, if the people around you look the other way. How others react – or do not react – to racism is a big part of the experience.

As we've explored earlier, looking at racism can make some people (mainly white people) uncomfortable. And so they find reasons to justify what has happened to you, reasons to pretend that it's a total coincidence that has nothing to do with the colour of your skin, reasons to explain why this ugly and embarrassing thing wasn't actually racism. Every one of those reasons calls your reality into question, making it easy to begin to doubt yourself and wonder whether you're just imagining things. This process is called gaslighting.

Gaslighting is scary, especially when people with power over us – like teachers or parents – do it. And even though it has damaging results, gaslighting is a pretty typical response to racism. That seed of doubt makes people of colour less likely to speak up about the racism we experience to avoid the risk of not being supported, meaning that white people are less likely to feel like they should change any part of their lives (e.g. who they're friends with) as a result of having racism brought to their attention.

Remember: you are not imagining things. Racism exists in this world, no matter how many people want to pretend it doesn't. And the only way to change the world for the better is by acknowledging and challenging racism. It's alright to take a step back from people who are racist towards you or other people, and it's alright to do the same with people who gaslight. On the pages that follow, we'll look at how you can challenge racism when it occurs, as well as what people can do to unlearn racist attitudes.

Claire Heuchan

HOW CAN YOU CHALLENGE RACISM?

It's important to challenge racism if you ever witness it. You may see it in many different places. On the street, in the playground, in the classroom, at home, or on our screens. As you've seen in the 'my experience' pieces throughout the book, racism takes place everywhere: from hotels, to schools, to your home, to the street, to the classroom, to your own mind.

Here are some ways you can challenge it if you witness it:

ON THE STREET

If you see or hear someone abusing someone else because of the colour of their skin, or if you feel like someone is discriminating against a person because of their race, it's important to do two things: one is to be a good ally to the person being abused and/or discriminated against. The other is to challenge the discriminator/abuser. (It's important, in this instance to just remind you to consider your own safety at all costs. Only intervene if you feel safe to do so.)

Being a good ally: The person who is being abused or discriminated against will need support, whether it's emotional support or help removing themselves from a bad situation. It's important that you are encouraging and ensure they do not feel like being on the receiving end of racist abuse is in any way their fault. It's important that they do not blame themselves. Help them by making them feel it was not their fault. You can even help them report it and offer to be a witness if you saw what happened.

Challenging the discriminator: Again, we must reiterate, only do this if you feel safe to do so and the victim has been suitably removed from the situation. Tell the person to stop, that what they said was discriminatory and remind them that not only is what they did illegal but it is also inhumane.

IN THE HOME

You may hear a teacher or a relative expressing racist views. It is important to challenge these because that person may not realise the impact of their words. Sometimes the comment can be a casual thing that invokes a stereotype. Other times it could come from a place of ignorance or misunderstanding. In which case, it is your duty to inform your relative or teacher or classmate that what they said was racist. Don't call them a racist. There is a big difference between calling someone a racist and telling someone what they said was racist. By telling someone what they said was racist and explaining why, you are giving them an opportunity to learn, reflect and change their behaviour. Calling someone a racist can make them defensive and more entrenched in their beliefs, and it then becomes difficult to have a constructive conversation.

ON OUR SCREENS

If you see something on television, in a film, an advert or on a website that you think holds racist views, you can do something about it. It is important to realise that people are entitled to their opinions and some people may hold very different views to you. However, if you feel that the views reflected in a television programme, a film or an advert are racist and have concerns about whether they constitute hate speech, you can report them and the relevant authorities will carry out an investigation. There are contact details on page 47.

THINK ABOUT

What can you do, provided it's safe for you, to challenge racism? Does it make you feel nervous, hopeful, or a bit of both? Why is that?

If you see something on screen that you think has racist content, there are websites where you can report it.

UNLEARNING
RACISM

Racism is a sneaky thing – the more we pretend it isn't there or we can't see it, the more harm it is allowed to do. It's so deeply embedded in our society that we don't always recognise racism for what it is, or realise that the name for what we see happening in front of us is racism.

People of colour internalise racism, meaning that on some level we learn to believe parts of the prejudices that get projected on to us – like the Doll Test (see pages 32-33) shows. White people learn how to use it against people of colour in damaging ways, sometimes deliberately and other times subconsciously. We saw on pages 17 and 27 how white people have used racism in ways that lets them get ahead or secure their position in life.

We learn racism from an early age, soaking it in through our history, culture and media. This means that racism can seem like a normal part of life: 'just the way things are'. The good news is that we don't have to accept social inequality as a normal part of society. Better still: we don't have to accept racism as part of how we think, because each of us has the power to change and grow. We have the ability to unlearn racism.

Unlearning racism is one of the most useful things you will ever do. It can change the world, and that change starts from within.

For people of colour, unlearning racism means repairing some of the damage that comes from living in an environment that can be hostile. It means learning to love the colour of your skin, the texture of your hair, the shape of your nose and everything about yourself that has ever been treated like it's wrong because it's different to white features. To unlearn racism is to stop measuring yourself against the standards set by whiteness. It can build your confidence, self-worth and happiness.

For white people, unlearning racism means questioning where the assumptions you make about people of colour are coming from, and questioning why you make those assumptions in the first place. It means recognising the ways your race makes your life easier instead of harder, the way it would affect you if you were a person of colour. Unlearning racism means never using it against a person of colour for any reason. Unlearning racism means being willing to give up the perks that come with white skin, like the way you are more likely to be hired for a job than a person of colour with the same skills and qualifications and paid more than people of colour in the same role. Giving up privilege can be scary, especially when it makes our day-to-day lives that much easier, but it's an important step towards building a fairer world for everyone to live in.

THINK ABOUT

What can you do to unlearn racism in your own life?

"The mess we are living in is a deliberate one. If it was created by people, it can be dismantled by people, and it can be rebuilt in a way that serves all."

Reni Eddo-Lodge, writer

WHAT DO YOU THINK?

Now that you've read the book, have your thoughts on race and racism changed? What about your opinion on whether or not skin colour matters?

Talking About Race

What does talking about race make you feel? Why might that be? Can you think of reasons people shy away from discussing race?

Recognising Racism

Why is it important to know if something is racist? Can you think of a reason why different people might have different opinions about whether or not something is racist? How does being able to recognise racism help us to challenge it?

Racist Structures

What consequences do you think it has when an organisation, like a school or club, doesn't have any way for the people who are part of it to speak out about racism? How do you think racism shapes the way organisations work?

What if I've Said or Done Something Racist?

What do you think is the best thing to do if you realise you might have been racist towards someone? Why is it important to think more about their feelings than your own when deciding how to move forward?

"I remember being in a history lesson and saying to my teacher, 'How come you never talk about black scientists and inventors and pioneers?' And she looked at me and said, 'Because there aren't any.'"

Malorie Blackman, writer

GLOSSARY

British Empire Britain and its 'colonies', the countries it ruled. At its height in 1922 it governed a fifth of the global population and a quarter of the world's land area

consent agreement to an action that would otherwise not respect a person's boundaries

default automatic or expected position

dehumanise to fail or refuse to recognise the human dignity of another person

discriminate to treat an individual or group differently, usually in a negative way, because of their identity

entrenched describes something that is deeply rooted

erasure the deliberate removal of people from the stories that make up culture, history and group identity

ethnicity the cultural background of a person

hate speech language used to abuse or shame people in response to their identity

homophobia bigotry towards gay men and lesbian women, a fear or hatred of men who love men and women who love women

institutional racism racism that's woven into how systems are organised, e.g. government or education, and shapes the workings of society

lynching a form of public execution traditionally used to kill black people, particularly in North America

prejudice an irrational feeling of dislike towards a group

privilege a form of power (quite often taken for granted by those who hold it)

social norms the identities or values that are treated as what's normal in society – not looked at as different or even suspicious, but accepted as typical

stereotype a set of ideas attached to a particular identity, coming from a place of prejudice rather than facts

talisman an item we think of as lucky, or a token of something we care about

white supremacy the system that treats white people as human and people of colour as less than human; the thinking behind racism

FURTHER INFORMATION

WEBSITES

The Equality Advisory and Support
equalityadvisoryservice.com
The EASS has a website and helpline (0808 800 0082) offering advice on issues relating to equality and human rights.

Advertising Standards Authority **asa.org.uk**
The ASA describes itself as the UK's independent regulator of advertising across all media. Its website offers guidance of making a complaint.

Coalition for Racial Equality and Rights (CRER) **www.crer.scot**
CRER does brilliant work campaigning against racial inequality in Scotland.

Ofcom **ofcom.org.uk**
Contact Ofcom to complain about, or report, issues relating to TV or radio programmes.

BOOKS

Racism and Intolerance (Children in Our World series) Louise Spilsbury and Hanane Kai, Wayland, 2018

Questions and Feelings About Racism Anita Ganeri and Ximena Jeria Franklin Watts, 2018

Young, Gifted and Black: Meet 52 Black Heroes from Past and Present Jamia Wilson and Andrea Pippins Wide Eyed Editions, 2018

INDEX